I0817004

HISTORY OF HOLIDAYS AND FESTIVALS

INDIGENOUS PEOPLES' DAY

BY HEATHER L. BODE

Core Library

An Imprint of Abdo Publishing
abdobooks.com

Cover image: At Indigenous Peoples' Day events, people often wear traditional clothing featuring materials such as feathers and beads.

abdobooks.com

Published by Abdo Publishing, a division of ABDO, PO Box 398166, Minneapolis, Minnesota 55439.

Printed in China.
102023
012024

Cover Photo: Giordanno Brumas/SOPA Images/Sipa USA/Alamy
Interior Photos: Steve Russell/Toronto Star/Getty Images, 4–5; Joseph Prezioso/AFP/Getty Images, 6; Alex Wong/Getty Images News/Getty Images, 10; Red Line Editorial, 12, 36; Metropolitan Museum of Art, 14–15; Everett Collection/Shutterstock Images, 17; Smith Archive/Alamy, 21, 45; Wisconsin Historical Society/Archive Photos/Getty Images, 24–25; Bettmann/Getty Images, 29; Soloman Kargin/Pix/Michael Ochs Archives/Getty Images, 30; Paul Sakuma/AP Images, 32, 43; David McNew/Getty Images News/Getty Images, 34–35; Luke E. Montavon/AFP/Getty Images, 38; Anna Moneymaker/Getty Images News/Getty Images, 40

Editor: Laura Stickney
Series Designer: Ryan Gale

Library of Congress Control Number: 2023939631

Publisher's Cataloging-in-Publication Data
Names: Bode, Heather L., author.
Title: Indigenous Peoples' Day / by Heather L. Bode
Description: Minneapolis, Minnesota: Abdo Publishing, 2024 | Series: History of holidays and festivals | Includes online resources and index.
Identifiers: ISBN 9781098292614 (lib. bdg.) | ISBN 9798384910558 (ebook)
Subjects: LCSH: Holidays--Juvenile literature. | Festivals--Juvenile literature. | Indigenous Peoples' Day--Juvenile literature. | Native American Day--Juvenile literature. | Indians of North America--Juvenile literature.
Classification: DDC 394.264--dc23

CONTENTS

CHAPTER ONE

A VOICE FOR THE PEOPLE

Every year, the city of Berkeley, California, hosts the Indigenous Peoples' Day Powwow. Both Indigenous and non-Indigenous people wander the market. It is filled with booths displaying artwork, clothing, and food. Fry bread, a type of deep-fried flatbread, sizzles in hot oil. Indigenous dancers dressed in handmade regalia walk by. Metallic cones sewn in rows jingle on dresses. Beads on moccasins glisten. Headdresses crowned with

Powwows often feature dances from a variety of Indigenous nations. One is the Hoop Dance, in which dancers tell a story using up to 30 hoops.

Traditional Indigenous regalia may include feather headdresses, porcupine quills, handmade jewelry, colorful fabrics, moccasins, and ribbons.

eagle feathers stand tall above the crowd. Musicians take their seats around a drum.

The day's host is Randy Pico, of the Luiseno people. He says the Indigenous Peoples' Day Powwow is like a homecoming. People come to see friends from near and far. Pico welcomes everyone to the powwow. Then the festivities begin with land acknowledgment.

This moment honors American Indian nations that originally inhabited the land on which the celebration is being held. Berkeley's annual celebration is held on the land of the Ohlone people.

Pico tells the crowd that every day is a good day to be Indigenous. Then the city's mayor proclaims the day Indigenous Peoples' Day. Drums beat in rhythm as voices rise in song. Members of the Luiseno, Ohlone, Blackfeet, and other nations join hands to form a circle. Dancers bend their knees and sidestep in time to the drums. In this circle, all nations are welcomed.

WHAT IS INDIGENOUS PEOPLES' DAY?

Indigenous Peoples' Day is a holiday celebrated on the second Monday of October. It aims to honor the cultures and contributions of Indigenous peoples in the past, present, and future. Long before Europeans arrived in what is now North America, Indigenous nations lived on the land. They held special knowledge of food, natural resources, building materials, and medicinal plants.

Indigenous Peoples' Day celebrates the strength of Indigenous nations. The European colonization of the Americas, which began in 1492 and lasted into the 1700s, forced Indigenous people from their homelands. But Indigenous nations continue to survive and thrive. Today, there are 574 federally recognized nations in the United States.

The holiday helps educate people about issues that American Indians face. Every ten years, the country counts its population. This is called taking a census. In the 2020 census, 2.9 percent of US citizens registered as American Indian or Alaska Native. About 9.7 million people registered as American Indian and Alaska Native alone, or in combination with other races.

American Indian communities suffer from poverty, domestic violence, and low educational achievement. These issues impact their communities at a higher rate than people of other ethnicities. Their ways of living forever changed after the US government forced Indigenous people from their homelands.

American Indians also tend to be underrepresented in what people see, hear, and read. People often form cultural views based on what they see on television, in movies, or in books. Without accurate representations of American Indians, many people hold stereotypical views. This can impact how

PERSPECTIVES

VOICES FOR THE FUTURE

Dylan O. Baca is from the White Mountain Apache Tribe and Navajo Nation. In 2019, he founded Indigenous Peoples' Initiative. This youth-led organization helps promote Indigenous Peoples' Day. It helped the White House draft a presidential proclamation recognizing the holiday. President Joe Biden signed the proclamation in 2021. On the organization's website, Baca says, "When historians sit down and pick up their pens to write the story of the 21st century, let it be our generation, who laid down the heavy burden of hate and let peace triumph over violence and hatred."

Many people fight to raise awareness about issues that Indigenous communities face. People take part in protests, marches, and other demonstrations.

American Indians see themselves. Indigenous Peoples' Day helps people hear accurate narratives about the lives of Indigenous people today.

BECOMING A HOLIDAY

As of 2022, Indigenous Peoples' Day was not a federal US holiday. A bill proposed in 2021 must pass in order to make it one. But even before the bill, some state and local governments were officially celebrating the holiday. In 1990, South Dakota was the first state to celebrate it. South Dakota called it Native Americans' Day. People gathered at Crazy Horse Memorial and Custer State Park, landmarks in the Black Hills of South Dakota. The Black Hills are considered sacred land by the Lakota, Northern Cheyenne, and Omaha peoples.

By 2022, ten states officially celebrated Indigenous Peoples' Day. Another ten states, along with Washington, DC, observed it by proclamation. This means they made an

FEDERAL HOLIDAYS

In the United States, a holiday is a day that honors an event or a person. Some holidays are closely tied to religious practices. Others are related to the nation's history. Federal holidays are declared by the government. These days are recognized by the US Congress. On federal holidays, people may have the day off from school or work. Federal US holidays include Christmas Day, New Year's Day, Memorial Day, Columbus Day, and Veterans Day.

INDIGENOUS PEOPLES' DAY BY STATE

In 2022, several states celebrated or observed Indigenous Peoples' Day. Why do you think certain regions of the country officially celebrate the holiday while others do not?

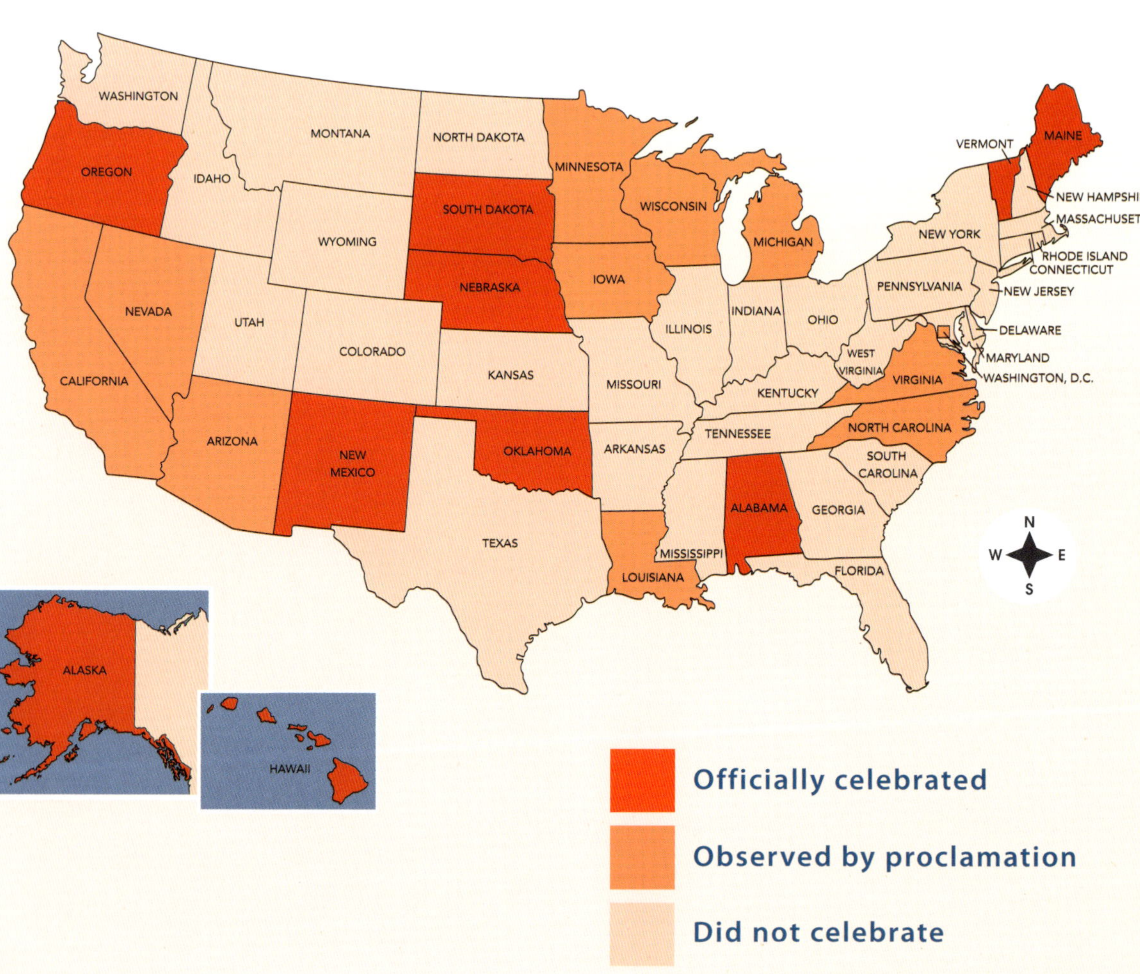

announcement in support of celebrating the holiday. In 2022, 100 cities around the country also celebrated it.

Different states and cities celebrate Indigenous Peoples' Day with a variety of events, including music, dances, nature walks, and food tastings. Museums put on special displays and exhibits. Tribal leaders may give speeches or lead discussions about current issues. There is much diversity in how the holiday is celebrated, just as there is much diversity among Indigenous nations.

EXPLORE ONLINE

Chapter One talks about how Indigenous Peoples' Day is celebrated in the United States. The website below gives more information about Indigenous Peoples' Day. How is this information the same as the information in Chapter One? What new information did you learn from the website?

INDIGENOUS PEOPLES' DAY

abdocorelibrary.com/indigenous-peoples-day

LIGVRIS · MIRANDA · COLVMBI · ANTIPODV
PENETRAVIT · IN · ORBEM ·

CHAPTER TWO

EARLY HISTORY

Indigenous people live all over the world. In the United States, Indigenous people are often called Native Americans or American Indians. The word *Indian* is connected to a man named Christopher Columbus.

Columbus was an Italian explorer. The king and queen of Spain funded his voyages. Columbus had three ships and a crew of 80 to 90 men. In 1492, Columbus and his crew left Spain and sailed across the Atlantic Ocean. They hoped to find a water route to the

Christopher Columbus was given the title "Admiral of the Ocean Sea" by the king and queen of Spain.

Indian Ocean. They landed in a group of islands now known as Hispaniola, the Bahamas, and Cuba. These lie in the Atlantic Ocean south of Florida. While the exact location of Columbus's landing is unknown, the Indigenous people who lived there called it Guanahani. It was home to the Taino people. Columbus believed he had reached the Indies, or regions of Asia. So he called the people who lived there "Indians."

In 1493, Columbus wrote to the king and queen about the land. He wanted to claim the land for Spain. He also wanted gold and other resources such as cotton. The Taino people had access to these resources.

At the time of Columbus's arrival, the Taino population was likely between 1 and 4 million. The Taino welcomed Columbus. They offered him gifts such as parrots and cotton. But what seemed to be a friendly relationship quickly changed. The Europeans carried diseases that were new to the Taino. The Taino had no immunity to diseases such as smallpox and influenza. These diseases caused many Taino people to die.

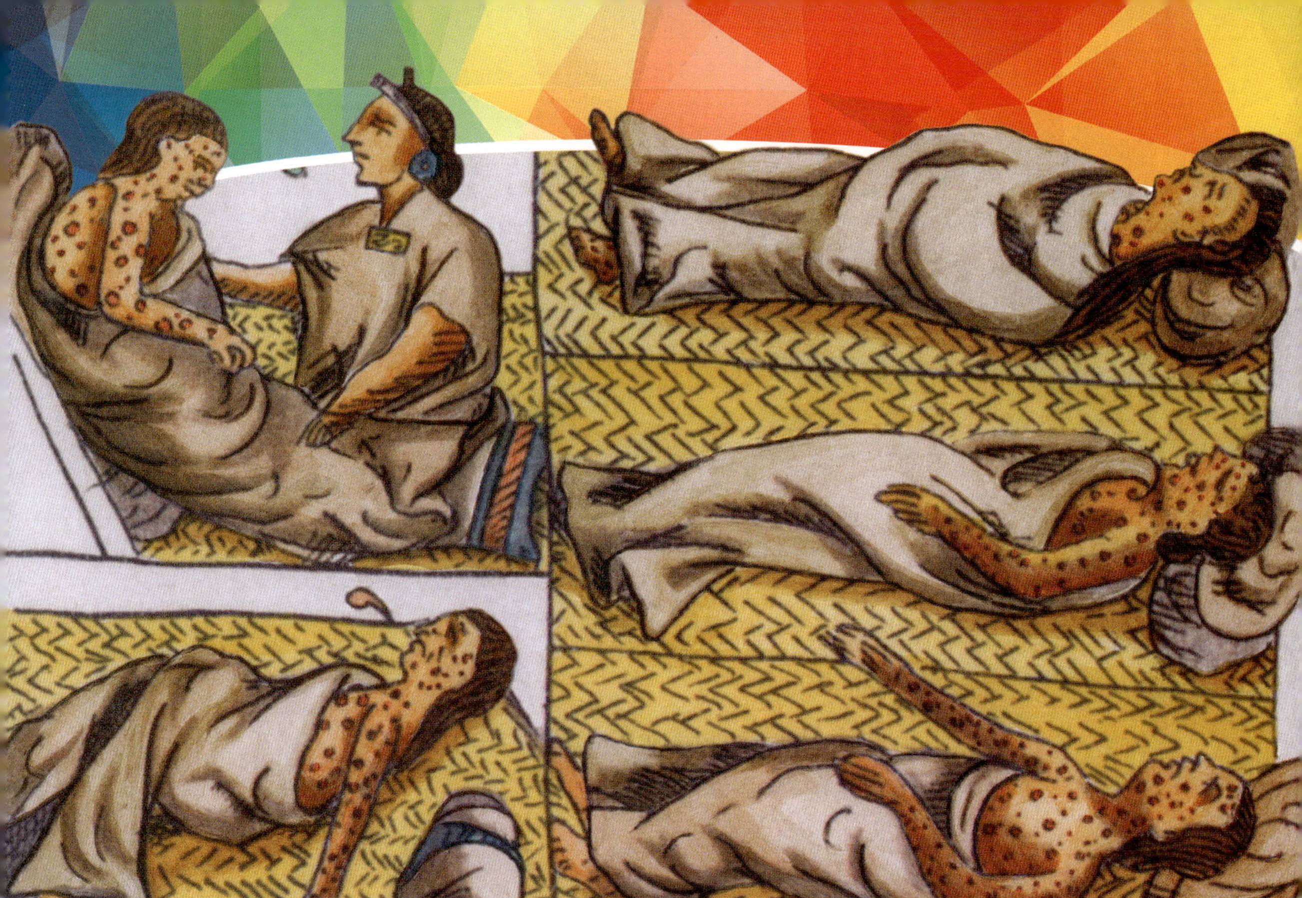

One of the deadliest diseases that European explorers brought to the Americas was smallpox. It caused fever, vomiting, painful blisters, and often death.

Columbus also forced the Taino people to pay him gold every three months. When the Taino could not pay, many ran away to the mountains. Others were kidnapped and forced into slavery by Columbus and his men. When the Taino population became too small, Columbus brought enslaved people from Africa to continue their work.

EUROPEANS ARRIVE

After Columbus's voyage, other Europeans sailed across the Atlantic Ocean to North America. They came from three main countries: Spain, France, and England. The Spanish wanted to convert Indigenous people to their religion. They also wanted slave laborers for their silver mines and large farms. Spain established the cities of Saint Augustine, Florida, in 1565 and Santa Fe, New Mexico, in 1609.

France wanted access to inland waterways in North America. This would give them control of the fur trade. France established Canadian cities such as Québec City in 1608 and Montréal in 1642.

The English established Jamestown, Virginia, in 1607 and Plymouth, Massachusetts, in 1620. They planned to colonize the land. This meant taking over the land. It did not mean living peacefully as neighbors.

In 1776, the 13 English colonies declared their independence from the king of England. By 1783, the colonies had won their independence and become a new country, the United States of America. After 1790, the US government often forced the Indigenous people who lived in these lands to move. Or they attempted to assimilate Indigenous people into their cultures. This practice covered many areas of life, including religion, language, education, and cultural celebrations. Many Indigenous nations blended Christianity into their religions. They learned to speak English. Some Indigenous people married enslaved African people or white settlers.

RESERVATIONS

In 1851, the US Congress passed the Indian Appropriations Act. This created the reservation system. American Indians were forced to move to reservations. Many nations lost their traditional food sources. Their ability to hunt and fish was restricted. Some reservations received food rations. But these shipments of food sometimes arrived rotten or moldy. American Indians were also not used to ingredients like flour, sugar, and beef. This led to sickness, starvation, and malnutrition.

TREATIES

Over the years, Indigenous people made treaties with European nations. Treaties were, and still are, important. Many American Indians believe words are sacred. All promises, spoken and written, are to be kept. Treaties are also legal documents. Their purpose changed over time. At first, trade was set up through alliances, or formal agreements with other nations. For example, the French wanted access to Algonquin, Huron, and Montagnais land for fur trapping. In exchange, the French offered these nations guns and cloth.

As European nations fought to dominate North America, treaties were used to form alliances in case of war. These were written agreements between sovereign nations, or nations that rule themselves. After the United States was formed, it made treaties as well. The 1778 Treaty with the Delaware Nation said the United States and the Delaware would protect each other against the British. But over the years, the US government often made treaties and then broke them.

More than 100 tribal leaders from the Lakota and Arapaho nations signed the Fort Laramie Treaty of 1868.

Another common purpose for treaties involved land. As more Europeans arrived and settled in North America, they wanted to have more land. The 1784 Treaty of Fort Stanwix established land boundaries between the United States and the Six Nations of the Seneca, Mohawk, Onondaga, Cayuga, Oneida, and Tuscarora.

PERSPECTIVES

AMERICAN INDIAN BOARDING SCHOOLS

Between 1869 and the 1960s, the government took many Indigenous children from their families and forced them to attend boarding schools. They were not allowed to speak their languages. They had to cut off their long hair, a source of pride for many American Indians. Lone Wolf, of the Blackfeet, went to Fort Shaw Indian School. He said, "Once there our belongings were taken from us, even the little medicine bags our mothers had given us to protect us from harm. Everything was placed in a heap and set afire. . . . If we thought the days were bad, the nights were much worse. That was the time when real loneliness set in, for it was then we knew that we were all alone."

Under the Fort Laramie Treaty of 1868, the Lakota and Arapaho nations gave up thousands of acres of land. In return, they would have hunting and fishing rights in the areas they gave up. Under the treaty, they moved onto a reservation in the Black Hills. But the treaty was broken when white gold seekers invaded the Black Hills. Events like this caused mistrust between Indigenous nations and the United States.

STRAIGHT TO THE SOURCE

For hundreds of years, Indigenous nations faced the arrival of white settlers. Many tribal elders predicted their coming and said it would change life forever. Here, Black Elk, a member of the Oglala Sioux, tells a story he heard from his father:

> *There was once a Lakota (Sioux) holy man, called Drinks Water, who dreamed what was to be; and this was long before the coming of the Wasichus (white men). He dreamed that the four-leggeds were going back into the earth and that a strange race had woven a spider's web all around the Lakotas. And he said: 'When this happens, you shall live in square gray houses, in a barren land, and beside those square gray houses you shall starve.'*

Source: Peter Nabokov, editor. *Native American Testimony: An Anthology of Indian and White Relations: First Encounter to Dispossession*. Crowell, 1978.

BACK IT UP

The author of this passage is using evidence to support a point. Write a paragraph describing the point the author is making. Then write down two or three pieces of evidence the author uses to make the point.

CHICAGO STORE

CHAPTER THREE

THE ROLE OF ACTIVISM

In 1792, 300 years after Columbus's arrival, New York City celebrated Columbus Day. By the late 1800s, Italian immigrants in the United States faced racial attacks. Some Americans feared immigrants would take their jobs. Because Italians had darker skin tones, they stood out as a target. In 1891, 11 Italian immigrants were killed in New Orleans. In 1892, President Benjamin Harrison proclaimed a special one-time holiday to thwart anti-Italian American feelings. It was called Columbus Day.

In 1892, some US cities celebrated Columbus Day with parades. It was the 400th anniversary of Columbus's landing.

KEEP TALKING ABOUT COLUMBUS?

Ben Pease of the Crow and Northern Cheyenne peoples is an artist and cofounder of Indigenous Peoples' Day Montana. Pease uses his art as a voice for change. He says the driving force behind Indigenous Peoples' Day is accurate education. His organization aims to celebrate and normalize diversity. He says, "A lot of people say, 'We shouldn't say Columbus anymore. He Whose Name We Shall Not State.' I think we should continue saying the name in some ways. Say why we shouldn't forget. Say that Columbus and many of his men and other explorers were bad players: war mongering, murder, child slavery."

In 1934, President Franklin D. Roosevelt proclaimed the first national observance of Columbus Day. It was a day to celebrate Italian American heritage and remember Columbus. But people still worked and went to school. Columbus Day became a national holiday in 1937.

SPEAKING OUT

To fight against years of mistreatment and discrimination, many people began speaking up in support of Indigenous people. In 1923, Deskaheh, chief of the Iroquois Confederacy, traveled to Geneva, Switzerland. He hoped to attend a League of Nations meeting. The League of Nations brought world leaders together to discuss global issues. Deskaheh wrote a letter asking the League of Nations to recognize the sovereignty of the Iroquois Confederacy. But the League of Nations refused to hear him.

Later, several activist groups began fighting for American Indians. In 1968, the American Indian Movement (AIM) began in Minneapolis, Minnesota. Leaders of this organization included Dennis Banks of the Anishinaabe, Russell Means of the Oglala Lakota, and Clyde H. Bellecourt of the Ojibwe. They fought for treaties to be honored and for Indigenous land to be returned. AIM also helped raise awareness about the high poverty and unemployment rates of American Indians.

In 1969, a group of Indigenous students led by Richard Oaks of the Mohawk Nation took over

Alcatraz Island. This island is off the coast of California. Formerly a prison, it had been abandoned six years earlier. Some treaties gave tribes the right to reclaim abandoned government property if it was within their original territory. Indigenous people from the area believed Alcatraz Island belonged to them. They hoped to turn the island into a cultural center. The occupation lasted for about 18 months. It ended when government officials cut off the island's water and electrical supply. But media coverage of the Alcatraz occupation helped draw attention to issues impacting Indigenous societies. It gave Indigenous nations a new sense of dignity and pride in their cultures.

Later, the League of Nations was replaced by the United Nations (UN). In 1977, the UN held a special meeting. It focused on discrimination against Indigenous peoples around the world. This is where the idea of Indigenous Peoples' Day was first proposed.

In 1990, the UN held a conference called the International Conference on Discrimination against

AIM leaders including Russell Means and Dennis Banks spoke out against the mistreatment of American Indians. They led protests, raising awareness about issues such as treaty rights and racism.

Indigenous Populations in the Americas. At this conference, people discussed replacing Columbus Day with Indigenous Peoples' Day. Later in the year, the Continental Gathering of Indigenous Peoples met in

Thousands of American Indians took part in the 1969 Alcatraz occupation. Some of them painted peaceful messages and symbols around the island, reclaiming it as their land.

Quito, Ecuador. At this meeting, people also discussed the idea of Indigenous Peoples' Day. The timing of these discussions was important. This is because 1992 marked the 500th anniversary of Columbus's landing.

In 1992, the city of Berkeley, California, planned Indigenous Peoples' Day. It wanted to protest the celebration of Columbus Day. The city celebrated not only local Indigenous people, but also Indigenous people across the globe.

Today, Indigenous leaders around the world continue to promote the celebration of Indigenous Peoples' Day. They also voice concerns for the environment. Dennis Banks was one of the AIM leaders. He said that the land was always important. He encouraged his followers to always do what is best for

PERSPECTIVES

EDUCATION AS ACTIVISM

Activism takes on many forms. It can involve protests or political campaigns. But there are also other ways to create change. Amy Spotted Wolf of the Tohono O'odham and Hidatsa is an elementary educator. She sees education as a form of activism. "As an Indigenous person, I know my history and I know my students' histories, so this gives me an opportunity to teach them the truth," she says. "And although the truth of our histories can be very emotional . . . I am there to be there for them and comfort them and answer any questions that they have from a perspective of an Indigenous person, and not from a textbook or video."

1492-1992
AMERICAN INDIAN MOVEMENT
500 YEARS OF
RESISTANCE
PELICAN BAY
PRISON
COLUMBUS DISCOVERED AMERICA
NOT

the land. Topics like climate change and pollution are still very important to many Indigenous activists today. They continue to speak out about the misuse of natural resources such as water and oil. They fight to protect and honor the land.

FURTHER EVIDENCE

Chapter Three talks about how Indigenous nations continue to celebrate their cultures and promote the recognition of American Indians. Identify one of the chapter's main points. What evidence does the author provide to support this point? Read about the Mille Lacs Band of Ojibwe at the website below. Does the information support the main point of the chapter? Does it present new evidence?

HISTORY AND CULTURE

abdocorelibrary.com/indigenous-peoples-day

In 1992, Berkeley, California, became the first US city to celebrate Indigenous Peoples' Day. People celebrated 500 years of American Indian resistance.

CHAPTER FOUR

THE FUTURE OF INDIGENOUS PEOPLES' DAY

Today, Indigenous people live all over the United States. They live in rural areas, urban areas, and on reservations. Indigenous Peoples' Day celebrates the cultures of more than 600 sovereign Indigenous nations in the country. It makes Indigenous people from every unique nation visible.

Indigenous Peoples' Day is also a day to honor all Indigenous people who lost their lives and land because of colonization. The holiday helps educate non-Indigenous people

Today, the younger generations of Indigenous communities work to preserve their heritage and to support Indigenous rights. Many young people are involved in activist movements.

CURRENT ISSUES

One purpose of Indigenous Peoples' Day is to draw attention to current issues facing American Indians, such as poverty and unemployment. What do you think could be done to help solve these issues?

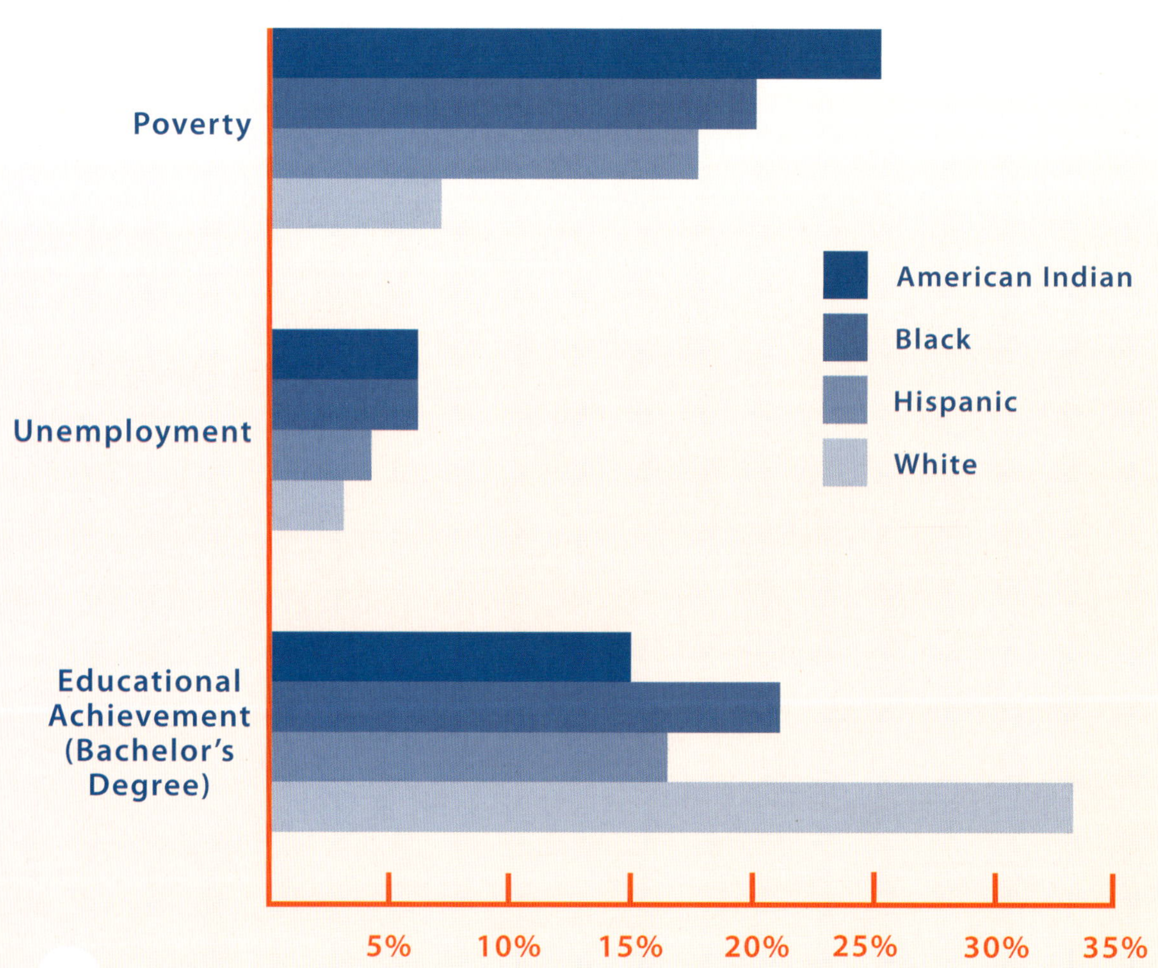

about Indigenous cultures. It also helps activists speak out about current issues impacting Indigenous people today.

REPLACE OR CELEBRATE?

Many people wonder if Columbus Day should be replaced by Indigenous Peoples' Day. Others wonder if both holidays should be celebrated together. Alaska, South Dakota, Vermont, and New Mexico recognize only Indigenous

PERSPECTIVES

GROWING UP WITH COLUMBUS DAY

MacKenzie Miettinen is from the Ojibwe Nation. She is an American Indian educator. She educates American Indian youth about their cultures. "I grew up when it was still Columbus Day, and Indigenous Peoples' Day was unheard of," she said. "It wasn't very clear for me as a student because at school my teachers would talk about how great Columbus was, but at home my family did the opposite. Now, with Indigenous Peoples' Day, hopefully our young Native students will have a different experience." She hopes her students will be proud of their cultures and see themselves reflected in mainstream society.

One way people can celebrate Indigenous Peoples' Day is by supporting Indigenous artists. Many cities hold American Indian art fairs and markets, where people can buy handmade goods such as artwork.

Peoples' Day. Other states, such as California and Nebraska, celebrate both holidays.

Some people believe celebrating both holidays denies history. They question whether Columbus should be celebrated with his own holiday. He caused hardship for many people. Some people think a good solution is to continue celebrating Italian Americans by honoring a different Italian, such as artist Leonardo da Vinci.

HOW TO CELEBRATE

There are many ways to celebrate Indigenous Peoples' Day. American Indians can engage their ethnic communities in discussion. They can invite speakers to events to help bring attention to current issues. Many people think Indigenous voices should shape the celebration. This may be through speeches or intertribal discussions.

Non-Indigenous people can celebrate the holiday too. They can attend Indigenous Peoples' Day events near their homes. They can research what nations lived or still live in their state. They can also think about ways to protect the environment.

CELEBRATING INDIGENOUS PEOPLES' DAY

In New Mexico, Indigenous Peoples' Day involves many activities. Grandmothers and grandfathers run races. Schoolchildren play games, such as a Zuni game with corn cobs or a Pueblo game that involves kicking a stick. They eat traditional food such as corn, mutton stew, and fry bread. Adults attend historical talks and movie screenings by Indigenous filmmakers. Voter registration booths ensure all voices are heard in US elections. Art shows exhibit Indigenous fashion, pottery, paintings, and other artwork. The Indian Market sells T-shirts and other products from small businesses. Many groups perform cultural singing and dancing, too.

On Indigenous Peoples' Day in 2021, hundreds of people called on President Joe Biden to pay attention to climate change and stop approving fossil fuel projects.

A NEW FEDERAL HOLIDAY?

On September 30, 2021, a bill was introduced in the US House of Representatives. This branch of Congress creates laws. Known as HR 5473, the bill sought to officially replace Columbus Day with Indigenous Peoples' Day. If passed, this law would make Indigenous Peoples' Day a federal holiday.

As the years go by, more cities and states are recognizing Indigenous Peoples' Day. This prompts debate over whether it should be a federal holiday. It provides an opportunity to recognize all Indigenous cultures and contributions around the country.

STRAIGHT TO THE SOURCE

On October 8, 2021, President Joe Biden gave his first Presidential Proclamation on Indigenous Peoples' Day:

> *Our country was conceived on a promise of equality and opportunity for all people—a promise that . . . we have never fully lived up to. That is especially true when it comes to upholding the rights and dignity of the Indigenous people who were here long before colonization of the Americas began. For generations, Federal policies . . . sought to assimilate and displace Native people and eradicate Native cultures. Today, we recognize Indigenous peoples' resilience and strength as well as the immeasurable positive impact that they have made on every aspect of American society. We also recommit to supporting a new, brighter future of promise and equity for Tribal Nations.*

Source: "Indigenous Peoples' Day, 2021." *Federal Register: The Daily Journal of the United States Government*, 8 Oct. 2021, federalregister.gov. Accessed 23 Feb. 2023.

WHAT'S THE BIG IDEA?

Take a close look at this passage. What can you tell about the connection between the government's history with Indigenous nations and its relationship with them today? Find specific words that refer to the past, present, and future.

IMPORTANT DATES

1492
Columbus travels from Spain searching for a water route to India. He lands near the Bahamas, home to the Taino people.

1492–1700s
European colonization of the Americas begins.

1851
The Indian Appropriations Act makes the reservation system.

1923
Deskaheh, chief of the Iroquois Confederacy, travels to Geneva, Switzerland, to speak to the League of Nations.

1969
American Indian activism gains global attention through the occupation of Alcatraz Island.

1977
A UN conference discusses discrimination against Indigenous peoples. Indigenous Peoples' Day is first proposed.

1990

South Dakota becomes the first state to replace Columbus Day by law. It celebrates Native Americans' Day. The first Continental Gathering of Indigenous People is held.

2021

HR 5473 is brought to the House of Representatives. It seeks to make Indigenous Peoples' Day a federal holiday. President Biden issues a presidential proclamation recognizing Indigenous Peoples' Day.

STOP AND THINK

Tell the Tale

Chapter One describes an Indigenous Peoples' Day Powwow celebration. Imagine you are attending a powwow for the first time. Write 200 words describing the sights, sounds, smells, and tastes you experience.

Surprise Me

Chapter Two talks about Columbus's actions and treatment of the Taino people. After reading this book, what two or three facts about Columbus did you find most surprising? Write a few sentences about each fact. Why did you find each fact surprising?

Take a Stand

There are many ways to celebrate Indigenous Peoples' Day. Which way do you think would be most interesting and helpful for your friends, and why? How would you go about organizing a day to celebrate this holiday with them in this way?

Another View

Chapter Three discusses activism and its role in the development of Indigenous Peoples' Day. As you know, every source is different. Ask a librarian or another adult to help you find another source about Indigenous activist movements. Write a short essay comparing and contrasting the new source's point of view with that of this book's author. What is the point of view of each author? How are they similar and why? How are they different and why?

GLOSSARY

activism
a practice that encourages strong action to bring about change

assimilate
to absorb into another culture

colonization
settling in a land that was already inhabited by other people and claiming it as one's own

discrimination
the unequal treatment of people based on an observed difference, such as race

ethnic
belonging to a group of people who share a common cultural background

intertribal
involving members of more than one tribe

occupation
the act of holding or controlling an area by force

regalia
clothing worn by American Indians, royalty, or other groups for special occasions

stereotype
a simplified, widely held, often mistaken belief that people have about someone

ONLINE RESOURCES

To learn more about Indigenous Peoples' Day, visit our free resource websites below.

Visit **abdocorelibrary.com** or scan this QR code for free Common Core resources for teachers and students, including vetted activities, multimedia, and booklinks, for deeper subject comprehension.

Visit **abdobooklinks.com** or scan this QR code for free additional online weblinks for further learning. These links are routinely monitored and updated to provide the most current information available.

LEARN MORE

Gagne, Tammy. *Fact and Fiction of American Colonization.* Abdo, 2022.

Smith, Cynthia Leitich. *Ancestor Approved.* Heartdrum, 2021.

INDEX

About the Author

Heather L. Bode is an elementary educator who has taught in South Dakota, Montana, and Minnesota. She loves reading and writing nonfiction on high-interest topics. Other interests include travel and keeping up with her five children. She lives in Minneapolis, Minnesota.